MAN AS A PICTURE

OF

THE LIVING SPIRIT

RUDOLF STEINER

*Lecture given in London, 2nd September, 1923 on the
day of the foundation of the Anthroposophical Society
in Great Britain*

Translated by George Adams

Rudolf Steiner Press
London

First English edition 1952
Second edition 1972

Translated from a shorthand report unrevised by the
lecturer. The original text is included in the volume of the
Complete Edition of the works of Rudolf Steiner entitled:
Initiationswissenschaft und Sternenerkenntnis. (Bibl. No. 228.)
The volume contains the texts of eight lectures given by
Rudolf Steiner in different places between 27th July and
16th September, 1923.

This English edition of the following lecture is published
by permission of the *Rudolf Steiner-Nachlassverwaltung*,
Dornach, Switzerland.

I.S.B.N. 0 85440 253 5

MADE AND PRINTED IN GREAT BRITAIN BY
THE GARDEN CITY PRESS LIMITED
LETCHWORTH, HERTFORDSHIRE
SG6 1JS

The following lecture was given by Rudolf Steiner to an audience familiar with the general background of his anthroposophical teachings. He constantly emphasized the distinction between his written works and reports of lectures which were given as oral communications and were not originally intended for print. It should also be remembered that certain premises were taken for granted when the words were spoken. 'These premises,' Rudolf Steiner writes in his auto-biography, 'include at the very least the anthroposophical knowledge of Man and of the Cosmos in its spiritual essence; also of what may be called "anthroposophical history", told as an out-come of research into the spiritual world.'

* * *

A brief list of literature in English translation relevant to the content of the following lecture will be found at the end of the text, together with a summarized plan of the Complete Edition of the works of Rudolf Steiner in the original German.

My dear Friends,

After the excellent conference at Ilkley and summer school at Penmaenmawr, it gives me heartfelt pleasure to be able now to give this lecture at our London centre.

I may remind you first of what I said in former lectures here.* Man, in accomplishing his work from day to day and from year to year, works in the physical body which is given to him upon Earth, and through which he is physically linked with all earthly life. So long as we contemplate what surrounds us here in this physical existence upon Earth, including that which we ourselves contribute to it, we shall of course fix our attention mainly on the times we spend in waking life. Yet as I said in those earlier lectures, that which goes on for man during the times when he is fast asleep is still more important for his whole existence—even for what he is and does in earthly life.

When we look back in memory from any given

* See *Man's Life on Earth and in the Spiritual Worlds*. Six lectures given in England during 1922.

point in our life, we always exclude the times we spent asleep; we join the things we did and underwent by day and while awake, as though they were to form a continuous whole. Yet none of this would be possible without the intervening periods of sleep. Above all, if we want to know the true being of man, we must pay attention to these periods of sleep. A man might easily say that he knows nothing of what goes on during sleep. To ordinary consciousness this may seem true, but in reality it is not so. For if we had to look back into a life uninterrupted by sleep, we should be mere automata. True, we should still be spiritual beings, but we should be automata.

Even more important than the daily periods of sleep throughout our life are the times we spent in sleep as very little children. We retain the good effects of those early periods of sleep all through our life; in a sense, we only supplement them by what accrues to us spiritually night by night during the rest of life. If we came into the world as little children wide-awake and never slept, we should, once more, be automata; nay, in this automatic state we should be unable to do anything consciously at all. We should not even recognize what came about through us, as our own concern.

We may believe we have no memory at all of what transpires during sleep, but even that is not quite true. When we look back in memory, seeing the things we experienced while awake and omitting the periods of sleep, the fact is that we see a void, a nothing, in the intervals of time when we were sleeping. It is as though you were looking at a white wall where at one place the white paint was lacking; you see a black circle. Or there might be a hole with no light behind it; you see the empty hole inasmuch as you see darkness. So do you see the darkness when you look back on your own life. The times you spent asleep appear as darkness in the midst of life. And in reality it is to these darknesses of life that you say 'I.' If you did not see the darknesses you would have no consciousness of 'I.' You owe the ability to say 'I' to yourself, not to the fact that you were active every day from morning until night, but to the fact that you were also sleeping. The Ego as we know it in this earthly life is, to begin with, darkness of life, emptiness, even non-existence. If we consider our life truly, we shall not say that we owe our consciousness of self to the day but rather that we owe it to the night. This is the truth. It is

7

the night which makes us real human beings and no mere automata.

Indeed if we look back into earlier epochs of human evolution upon Earth, though he was no mere automaton even then, for he already had certain differences between his waking and sleeping states, yet inasmuch as he was more or less aware of his sleeping states even in ordinary waking life, man's earthly life and action was far more automatic than it is today.

Truth is, we never bring our real and inmost Ego with us from the spiritual world into the physical and earthly; we leave it in the spiritual world. Before we came down into earthly life it was in the spiritual world, and it is there again between our falling asleep and our awakening. It stays there always, and if by day—in the present form of human consciousness—we call ourselves an 'I,' this word is but an indication of something which is not here in the physical world at all; it only has its *picture* in this world.

We do not see ourselves aright if we say: 'Here am I, this robust and real man, standing upon Earth; here am I with my inmost being.' We only see ourselves aright if we say: 'Our true being is in the spiritual world, and what is here of us on Earth is but a picture—an image of our

8

true being.' It is entirely true if we regard what is here on Earth, not as the real man himself, but as the picture of the real man.

I will now shew how you can see this picture-character of man more clearly. Let us imagine ourselves asleep. The Ego is away from the physical and etheric body; the astral body too is away. Now it is the Ego which works in the blood of man and in his movements. In sleep the movements cease, inasmuch as the Ego is away; the blood however goes on working, and yet the Ego is not there. We need only think of the physical body and we must ask ourselves: What happens to it while we are asleep? Something must still be living and working in the blood, even as the Ego lives and works in it by day. Likewise the astral body, living as it does in the whole breathing process, leaves it by night, and yet the breathing goes on. Here again, something must be there within the breathing process, working in it even as the astral body does in waking life.

Thus every time we go to sleep, with our astral body we forsake those inner organs which are the organs of respiration, and with our Ego we forsake the pulsating forces of our blood. What then becomes of them by night? The answer is that while the man lies asleep in bed, Beings of the adjoining Hierarchy enter into the pulsating forces of the blood from which his Ego has departed. *Angels, Archangels and Archai* are then indwelling the self-same organs in which the human Ego dwells in waking life by day. Moreover in the breathing organs which we have forsaken inasmuch as the astral body is outside by night, Beings of the next higher Hierarchy—*Exusiai, Dynamis and Kyriotetes*—are living then.

Thus when we go to sleep at night, setting forth with our Ego and astral body, leaving behind the body of our waking life, Angels, Archangels and higher spiritual Beings enter into us and animate our organs while we are outside—until we re-awaken. And what is more, as to our ether-body, even in our day-waking life we are not able to fulfil what is needed there. The Beings of the highest Hierarchy—*Seraphim, Cherubim and Thrones*—have to indwell this ether-body even while we are awake; they remain there always.

Lastly the physical body; if we ourselves had to achieve all the great and wonderful processes taking place there, we should not merely do it very badly; we could not set about it at all. Here we are utterly helpless. What outer anatomy ascribes to the physical body could not even move a single atom of it. Powers of quite another order are required here, namely none other than those that have been known since primeval times as the supreme Trinity—the Powers of the *Father, Son and Holy Spirit*. They—the essential Trinity—indwell the physical body of man.

Therefore in truth, throughout our earthly life our physical body is not our own. If it depended on us, it could not go on at all. It is, as was said of old, the true Temple of the Godhead —of the Divine threefold Being. Likewise our ether-body is the dwelling-place of the Hierarchy of Seraphim, Cherubim and Thrones. They have to help in caring for the organs which are assigned to the etheric body. As to those physical and etheic organs on the other hand which are deserted every night by the astral body, they are provided for by the second Hierarchy— Kyriotetes, Dynamis and Exusiai. Lastly, the organs forsaken during sleep by the human Ego have to be cared for in the night by Angeloi, Archangeloi and Archai. There is a constant activity within the human being, proceeding not only from man himself. Only in waking life he lives in this bodily nature, so to speak, as a sub-tenant. For at the same time it is the Temple and the dwelling-place of spiritual Beings—the Beings of the Hierarchies.

Bearing all this in mind, we only see this outer form of man aright if we admit: It is a picture— a picture of the working-together of all the Hierarchies. They are within it. Look at this human head in all the detail of its form; look at the rest of the body in its human form. I do not look at it truly if I describe it as a reality—as a real being, thus or thus. I only look at it truly if I say: It is a *picture* of an invisible, super-sensible working of all the Hierarchies together. Only when things are seen in this way can one speak truly and in detail of what is commonly propounded in a rather abstract manner. The physical world is not the true reality, so it is said; it is a maya—the true reality is behind it. Yet such a statement does not help us much. It is too general, as if one were to say: Flowers are growing in the meadow. Just as this statement will only be of use if you know what kind of flowers, so too the knowledge of the higher world can only be applied in practice if one is able to point out in detail *how* it is working in the outer picture, maya, or reflection, which is its physical, sense-perceptible manifestation.

*　　　*　　　*

Man therefore, seen in his totality, both in his earthly life by day and in his earthly life by night, is related not only to his physical and visible environment on Earth but to a world of higher spiritual being. Through all the kingdoms of Nature upon Earth—mineral, plant, animal kingdom—there works what we may call a lower spiritual realm. So too throughout the world of stars there works a higher spiritual realm—a realm which also influences man. Looked at in his totality, man is related through his physical existence to plants and animals, to water and to air; so too, he is related spiritually to the world of stars. The latter too is but a picture, a revelation of the underlying spiritual reality. It is the Beings of the Hierarchies who are really there. When he looks up to the stars, man in reality is looking up to the spiritual Beings of the Hierarchies. That which is raying down upon him is but a kind of symbolic light which they send to him of their presence, so that here too, even in physical life, he may have some indication of the living Spirit which in reality fills the entire Universe.

Just as on Earth we may long to know this mountain or that river, this animal or yonder plant, so should we feel a longing to get to know the starry world in its true being. In its true being it is spiritual. In Penmaenmawr I tried to tell a little of the real spiritual nature of the Moon, such as it shines upon us from the cosmic spaces in the present phase of earthly evolution. When we look up to the Moon, we never really see the Moon itself; we see at most a scanty indication of it where the illuminated crescent is continued. What we are seeing is the reflected sunlight, not the Moon itself. So altogether, only the cosmic forces thrown back or reflected by the Moon reach us upon Earth, never what lives within the Moon itself. That it reflects the Sun's light to the Earth is but a part, nay, the smallest part of what pertains to the Moon. All physical and spiritual impulses that reach it from the great Universe, the Moon reflects to us like a mirror. And as we never see through to the other side of a mirror, so do we never see the interior of the Moon, where, in effect, there lives a spiritual population among whom are very high guiding Beings. These guiding Powers, with the rest of the Lunar population, were once upon a time on Earth, whence they withdrew to the Moon more than 15,000 years ago. Before that time the Moon looked even physically different. It did not merely reflects the sunlight to the Earth but mingled in the sunlight something of its own essence. This is however not the point which interests us now. What does concern us at this moment is the fact that in the present epoch the Moon is there like a fortress in the Universe—a cosmic fortress within which lives a population which fulfilled its human destinies more than 15,000 years ago, and, with the spiritual guides of humanity, withdrew thereafter to the Moon. For there were once upon a time on Earth very advanced Beings—Beings who did not put on physical human bodies as do the men of today. They lived rather in etheric bodies, yet for the men who lived on Earth at that time they were the great leaders and educators.

It was these mighty teachers and educators who brought to mankind, long, long ago, the primeval wisdom—the original and sublime wisdom-teachings of mankind, whereof the Vedas, the Vendanta, are but a distant echo. They now are living in the Moon and only radiating spiritually to the Earth what issues from the Universe outside the Moon.

Something of the erstwhile Moon-forces has indeed remained behind on Earth, namely the physical forces of reproduction in man and animal; but that is all. Only the most external and physical element remained behind when at a certain time of old Atlantis the great teachers of mankind migrated to the Moon, which had itself withdrawn from the Earth long before.

Therefore when we look upward to the Moon we only see it truly if we realize that there are lofty spiritual Beings there—Beings who were once upon a time on Earth, and who now make it their task to ray down to Earth not what they bear within themselves, but the forces, both physical and spiritual, which they reflect and thus transmit from the great Universe. Whoever seeks Initiation-wisdom in present time, must among other things seek to receive into this Initiation-wisdom what the Beings of the Moon with their sublime spiritual forces have to tell.

Now this is only one of the 'cities' in the great Universe—one colony, one settlement among many. Others are no less important, notably those belonging to our planetary system. And as concerns ourselves—as concerns humanity on Earth—the other pole, the opposite extreme to the Moon, is the population of *Saturn*.

The Saturn population too, as you may gather from my *Occult Science*, was once united with the Earth, yet in a very different way from the population of the Moon. The Saturn-beings are

• •

connected with the earthly life in quite another way. They reflect nothing from cosmic space. Even the physical sunlight is only just reflected on to Earth by Saturn. Saturn like a lonely recluse wanders slowly round the Sun, shedding very little light. What outer Astronomy can tell us about Saturn is but a very small portion of the truth. The significance of Saturn for humanity on Earth is made manifest, if only in a picture, every night when man is sleeping, and it is realized more fully between death and new birth when man is going through the spiritual world— and therefore too through the world of stars—as I explained in a lecture here not long ago.*

True, in the present phase of evolution man does not meet Saturn directly; yet by a round-about way—which we need not go into now—he does come into contact with the Saturn-beings. Within Saturn in effect, Beings of high perfection, very sublime Beings live—Beings who are in near relation to Seraphim, Cherubim and Thrones. Seraphim, Cherubim and Thrones are as it were the Beings nearest to them—nearest among the Hierarchies.

The sublime Beings, whom we may call the Saturn population, do not ray down to Earth or

* See footnote page 5.

give to men from Saturn anything that can be found in the external, physical world. But they preserve the cosmic memory, the cosmic record. All facts and all events, both physical and spiritual, which the planetary system has undergone, all that the Beings within our planetary system have ever experienced—the Saturn-beings faithfully preserve it in memory. In recollection they are forever looking back on the entire life of the planetary system. Even as we look back in memory upon the limited range of our earthly life, so do the Saturn-beings—in their collective activity—cherish the cosmic memory of what the planetary system as a whole and all the beings in it have undergone.

For man himself, the spiritual forces living in this cosmic memory are present, inasmuch as he comes into relation with the Saturn-beings between death and a new birth, and also—more in picture-form—every night. Thereby the spiritual forces proceeding from the Saturn-beings—forces in which the deepest inner life of the planetary system is contained—are also working within man. Even as memory is our own deepest inner life on Earth, so too what lives in Saturn represents the innermost and deepest 'cosmic I' of the whole planetary system.

Inasmuch as these influences are also there in man, many things are going on in human life, of the significance of which we are for the most part quite unconscious—which none the less play the greatest imaginable part in our lives. What we are conscious of, is after all only a very small portion of our life.

Say for example there was an incisive moment, an all-important event in your life. You met another human being with whom you then went on through life together; or it was some other event, essential to your future life. If you look back in time from this event, you will be struck by the fact that something like a plan was leading you towards it, beginning long before. Something that happened, say, between your thirtieth and fiftieth year—follow it backward through your life and you will very likely find: 'I entered on the path leading to this event when I was ten or twelve years old; all that then followed was leading up to it, so that I landed there.'

Elderly people, looking back contemplatively upon their life, will find that it all works out. They will be able to say: 'There was a sub-conscious thread running through it all. Un-conscious forces were impelling me to the decisive events of my life.' These are the Saturn forces—forces implanted in us through our relation, such as has been indicated, to the 'inner population' of Saturn.

While therefore, of the Moon, only the physical forces of reproduction are there on Earth (for these are Lunar forces, once again, which remained at the Moon's departure), the very highest forces, namely the *cosmic moral forces,* are on Earth through Saturn. The source of cosmic equity, the great 'restorer of the balance' for all that happens upon Earth, is Saturn. And if the Moon-forces, now upon Earth, have to do only with heredity—heredity through father, mother and so on—the Saturn forces enter into human life through all that lives in Karma, from incarnation to incarnation. In this respect the other planets are intermediate between the two— they mediate between the physical upon the one hand and the highest ethical upon the other.

Jupiter, Mars and so on are there between Moon and Saturn. They in their several ways mediate what Moon and Saturn at the uttermost extremes bring into human life—the Moon inasmuch as its spiritual Beings have withdrawn, leaving behind with the earthly realm only the physical aspect, the physical force of propagation; and Saturn inasmuch as it represents the moral justice of the Universe in its highest aspect. These two are working together in that the other planets are there between them, weaving the one into the other. Karma through Saturn, physical heredity through the Moon: these in their interrelation shew how man upon his way from earthly life to earthly life is connected with the Earth itself and with the great Universe beyond the Earth.

As you will readily understand, my dear Friends, the science of today, fixing attention upon the earthly life alone, can only tell about a very little part of man. It tells a lot about the forces of heredity, yet even here it fails to see that these are Lunar forces left behind on Earth. It fails to relate them to the cosmic activities, transcending the mere earthly life, to which they properly belong. And it knows nothing at all about the destiny of Karma with which this earthly life is infused. Yet in reality, even as physical man is pulsated through and through by the living blood, so are the Beings bearing within them the vast memory of the planetary system with all its cosmic happenings, pulsating through man's Karma upon Earth. Looking into our own inner life, we must admit: We are true human beings only inasmuch as we have memory.

Looking out into the planetary system with all its physical and spiritual happenings, and reaching upward to Initiation-science, we must equally admit: This planetary system would be void of inner life were it not for the inhabitants of Saturn preserving through the ages the memory, the cosmic past thereof, and also pouring ever down into mankind the forces springing from this preservation of the cosmic past, whereby all human beings are immersed in a living spiritual-moral nexus of causes and effects leading from earthly life to earthly life.

*　　　*　　　*

In earthly life, as to his conscious action, man is confined—in his relation to other men—within narrow limits. But if he takes into account what he experiences between death and new birth, there his relation to other human beings, who like himself will be discarnate, living no longer in physical bodies, reaches far wider circles. True, between death and re-birth he is at one time more in the neighbourhood of the Lunar influences and at another more in the neighbourhood of those of Saturn, Mars and so on. Yet through the cosmic spaces the one kind of planetary force interpenetrates the other. As upon Earth we work from man to man across the narrow confines of terrestrial space, so between death and new birth there is a working from planet to planet. The Universe then becomes the scene of man's activity and of the mutual relations between men. There between death and new birth, maybe the one departed soul is in the realm of Venus while the other is in Jupiter's domain; yet the interactions between them are far more intimate and tender than is possible within the narrow confines of earthly life. And even as the cosmic distances are called into play, to be the scene of action of the relations between human souls between death and new birth, so too the Beings of the Hierarchies are there, working throughout the cosmic spaces. We have to tell not only of the working of the several kinds of Beings—say, the inhabitants of Venus, or of Mars. We have to tell of the *relations* between the populations of Mars and Venus—a never-ending interaction, a constant to and fro of spiritual forces between the population of Mars and that of Venus amid the Universe.

This which goes on in the Universe between the populations of *Mars* and *Venus*—this ever-living interplay in the spiritual Cosmos, the deeds of Mars and Venus fertilizing one another—all this again has its relation to man. Even as the

Saturn-memory is related to human Karma, and the physical Lunar forces, left behind on Earth, to the external force of reproduction, so is the hidden spiritual interaction between Mars and Venus related to what appears in earthly life as human speech. For we could never speak by virtue of physical forces alone. It is the eternal being of man, going on from earthly life to earthly life, living in effect between death and new birth, which radiates into this outer world the gift of speech. Whilst as a spiritual being we are on our way from death to a new birth, we come into the sphere of action of the mutually fertilizing life which goes on between Mars and Venus—between the spiritual populations of Mars and Venus. Their spiritual forces, raying to and fro, co-operating, enter also into us ourselves upon our way from death to a new birth. This too is reproduced on Earth as in a physical picture, out of the innermost being of man, entering into the organs of speech and song. Never should we be able to speak through these organs if they were not physically kindled by the forces we receive into the depths of our being between death and new birth—forces derived from what is ever streaming to and fro in the Cosmos between Mars and Venus.

Thus in our daily life and action we are under the influence of the same spiritual forces, to the outward signs of which we look up with awe and wonder when we look out into the starry heavens. He alone is able to look up with inner truth who knows that in the stars, raying down to us from cosmic space, are to be seen the signs and characters of the great cosmic writing. For they are but the written signs of the great Universe—of the eternal, all-embracing spiritual life and process which also lives within us and of which we, once more, are but the image.

Long, long ago, in an instinctive atavistic clairvoyance, mankind had vision and perception of these things. The vision faded. If he had kept it, man could never have grown free. The ancient vision was therefore darkened. In compensation, the Mystery of Golgotha came into earthly life. A sublime Being from the population of the Sun came to Earth. He could not, it is true, bring to mankind all at once a consciousness of what is going on in yonder world of stars, but He brought with Him the forces whereby this consciousness can gradually be achieved.

Therefore it happened that to begin with, while the Mystery of Golgotha was taking place, a Gnostic wisdom was still there, inherited from olden time, through which the Mystery was understood. This wisdom too then faded out; during the fourth century after Christ it vanished altogether. Yet the spiritual force which had come to Earth through Christ remained. Man can now call this force to life within him, if he once opens his eyes to the reality of spiritual worlds, as he can do through the communications of modern Spiritual Science.

How much is yet to come to the humanity of modern time through looking thus once more to spiritual worlds! It is a striking fact: yonder in Asia, in more than one Asiatic, Oriental country, are living those who still preserve some relic of the old instinctive wisdom. They are the educated people, the true scholars, in the Oriental sense. No doubt this remnant of an ancient wisdom no longer belongs, in the best sense of the word, to our time; it needs to be replaced by a more conscious wisdom. And yet these bearers of an ancient and instinctive wisdom look down with not a little contempt upon the people of Europe and America. They are persuaded that their ancient Oriental wisdom even in its decadence, even the remaining rags and tatters of it, are preferable to the kind of knowledge of which Western civilization is so inordinately proud.

Hence it is interesting to see a book recently published by a Cingalese, an Indian of Ceylon, *The Culture of Souls among the Western Nations*, wherein the author says to the Europeans, in effect: Since the Middle Ages your knowledge of the Christ has died out. No longer have you any real knowledge of the Christ, for he alone who can look up into the spiritual world can have real knowledge of the Christ. Hence you must first let teachers come to you from India, from Asia, to teach you Christianity again. You can actually read it in this book. A Cingalese Indian says to the Europeans: Teachers must come to you from Asia; they will be able to tell you what Christ really is. Your European teachers no longer know it. Since the decline of the Middle Ages you have lost your knowledge of the Christ.

Yet in reality it is for Europeans and Americans themselves once more to summon courage to look into the spiritual worlds from which the knowledge of the Christ, the wisdom of the Christ can be regained. Christ is the Being who came down from spiritual worlds into the earthly life. Therefore in His true inwardness He can only be understood in the light of the Spirit.

Upon this way it is also necessary for man to

learn to look upon himself as a picture—an image of the spiritual Beings, spiritual realities and activities, on Earth. And he can do so best of all by permeating himself with such ideas and perceptions as I presented to you at the beginning of this lecture. Amid his conscious experiences in the stream of time he looks into the emptiness. He becomes conscious that his true Ego never descends from the spiritual world; that in the physical world he is but a picture. The real 'I' is not here in the physical world at all. He sees, as it were, a hole in time—a seeming darkness—and it is to this that he says 'I'.

Man should therefore become aware of the deep significance of this fact. When he looks back and remembers his past life, he must admit: I see in memory the experiences I underwent from day to day, but there is ever and again a hole, a gap of darkness. It is this darkness which in my ordinary consciousness I call 'I'. But I must now become conscious of something more than this.

I have summed up this 'something more' in a few words, which—as a kind of meditation reaching out to the true 'I'—may be inscribed in the soul of every human being of our time. Ever repeatedly we may call to life in us these words of meditation, which I will write as follows:

28

Ich schaue in die Finsternis:
In ihr ersteht Licht—
Lebendes Licht.
Wer ist dies Licht in der Finsternis?
Ich bin es selbst in meiner Wirklichkeit!
Diese Wirklichkeit des Ich
Tritt nicht ein in mein Erdendasein.
Ich bin nur Bild davon.
Ich werde es aber wieder finden,
Wenn ich,
Guten Willens für den Geist,
Durch des Todes Pforte gegangen.

I gaze into the Darkness.
In it there arises Light—
Living Light!
Who is this Light in the Darkness?
It is I myself in my reality.
This reality of the 'I'
Does not enter into my earthly life.
I am but a picture of it.
But I shall find it again
When with good will for the Spirit
I shall have passed through the Gate of Death.

Entering ever and again into a meditative saying of this kind, we can confront the Darkness.

We realize that here on Earth we are only a picture of our true Being—that our true Being never comes down into the earthly life. Yet in the midst of the Darkness, through our good will towards the Spirit, a Light can dawn upon us, of which we may in truth confess: *This Light am I myself in my reality.*

Brief list of relevant Books and Lectures by Rudolf Steiner

Occult Science: an Outline
Verses and Meditations
Man as Symphony of the Creative Word
Macrocosm and Microcosm

All the published works of Rudolf Steiner in print in German and in English translation, as well as those by other authors on anthroposophical subjects, can be obtained from:

Rudolf Steiner Press
35 Park Road, London, NW1 6XT

COMPLETE EDITION

of the works of Rudolf Steiner in the original German. Published by the *Rudolf Steiner Nachlassverwaltung, Dornach, Switzerland*, by whom all rights are reserved. *General Plan* (abbreviated):

A. WRITINGS

I.   Works written between the years 1883 and 1925
II. Essays and articles written between 1882 and 1925
III. Letters, drafts, manuscripts, fragments, verses, inscriptions, meditative sayings, etc.

B. LECTURES

I.   Public Lectures
II. Lectures to Members of the Anthroposophical Society on general anthroposophical subjects
     Lectures to Members on the history of the Anthroposophical Movement and Anthroposophical Society
III. Lectures and Courses on special branches of work:
     Art: Eurythmy, Speech and Drama, Music, Visual Arts, History of Art
     Education
     Medicine and Therapy
     Science
     Sociology and the Threefold Social Order
     Lectures given to Workmen at the Goetheanum

The total number of lectures amounts to some six thousand, shorthand reports of which are available in the case of the great majority.

C. REPRODUCTIONS and SKETCHES

Paintings in water colours, drawings, coloured diagrams, Eurythmy forms, etc.

When the edition is complete the total number of volumes, each of a considerable size, will amount to several hundreds. A full and detailed *Bibliographical Survey*, with subjects, dates and places where the lectures were given, is available.

All volumes can be obtained from the Rudolf Steiner Press in London as well as directly from the *Rudolf Steiner Nachlassverwaltung* (address as above).